THE HOLOCAUST

Life and Death in the Camps

Jane Shuter

Heinemann Library
Chicago, Illinois

© 2003 Reed Educational & Professional Publishing
Published by Heinemann Library,
an imprint of Reed Educational & Professional Publishing,
Chicago, Illinois

Customer Service 888-454-2279

Visit our website at www.heinemannlibrary.com

Designed by Joanna Sapwell and Tinstar Design
Illustrations by Martin Griffin
Originated by Ambassador Litho Ltd
Printed in Hong Kong, by Wing King Tong

07 06 05 04 03
10 9 8 7 6 5 4 3 2 1

**Library of Congress
Cataloging-in-Publication Data**
Shuter, Jane.
  Life and death in the camps / Jane Shuter.
    p. cm. -- (The Holocaust)
Summary: Describes the living conditions endured by the
people taken to
concentration camps during the Holocaust, as well as their
chances of
survival.
Includes bibliographical references and index.
  ISBN 1-4034-0812-2 (HC), 1-4034-3204-X (Pbk.)
  1. Holocaust, Jewish (1939-1945)--Juvenile literature. [1.
World War,
1939-1945--Concentration camps. 2. Holocaust, Jewish
(1939-1945)] I.
Title. II. Holocaust (Chicago, Ill.)
  D804.34 .S639 2002
  940.53'18--dc21
                          2002006846

Acknowledgments
The author and publisher are grateful to the following for
permission to reproduce copyright material: pp. 4, 6, 13,
31 Mary Evans Picture Library; pp. 7, 9 Wiener Library; pp.
8, 34, 42, 43 Yad Vashem; pp. 10, 11, 15, 23, 26, 38, 40,
41 USHMM; pp. 12, 20 (top), 20 (bottom), 21 (top), 21
(bottom), 28, 35, 36 (1), 36 (2), 36 (3), 36 (4), 44 (top), 44
(bottom) Emma Robertson & Magnet Harlequin; pp. 14,
16, 17, 19, 22, 24, 27, 37, 45 Auschwitz-Birkenau State
Museum; p. 18 Dr. Roy Winkelman/Florida Center for
Instructional Technology; pp. 25, 39, 46 Mauthausen
Museum Archive; p. 29 Corbis; pp. 30, 32 Ullstein
Bilderdienst; p. 33 Mittel-Dora; p. 47 AKG.

Cover photograph shows female prisoners at Auschwitz
concentration camp just after liberation by the Soviet
Army on January 26, 1945, reproduced with permission
of USHMM.

Special thanks to Ronald Smelser and Sally Brown-Winter.

About the series consultants
Ronald Smelser is a history professor at the University
of Utah. He has written or edited eight books on the
Holocaust and over three dozen articles. His recent
publications include *Learning About the Holocaust: A
Student Guide* (4 vol.) and *Lessons and Legacies: The
Holocaust and Justice.* Professor Smelser is also a past
president of the German Studies Association.

Sally Brown-Winter has worked in the field of Jewish
Education as a principal and teacher for over 25 years.
In her schools, the Shoah—its history, lessons, and
implications—have been explored from kindergarten
through high school.

Some words are shown in bold, **like this.** You can find out what they mean by looking
in the glossary.

Contents

The Camp System

In 1933, the **Nazi** Party, led by Adolf Hitler, came to power in Germany. The Nazis wanted to create a new German empire, the **Third Reich.** This empire was to be far bigger than Germany, so it would have to take over other countries. The Nazis wanted the Third Reich to be full of Germans who would obey Hitler and the Nazis. They began to take action against anyone who might oppose them or who did not fit their idea of a German citizen.

Setting Up the Camp System

The Nazis began by arresting anyone they saw as a **political** opponent. They did not put these people in prison; instead they set up special prison camps. These camps were different from ordinary prisons because all of the prisoners in the camps were imprisoned without trial and had no date for their release. They lived and worked in appalling conditions and they died, or were killed, in large numbers.

The camps were very effective. By 1935, there were very few people left in Germany who were willing to oppose the Nazis openly. However, the Nazis did not close the camps. Instead, they started to fill them with various kinds of people whom they labeled **"undesirable."** The camps played a large part in the **Holocaust**—the deliberate and systematic attempt by the Nazis to kill all **Jewish** people in Nazi-controlled lands. We cannot be sure how many people died in the Holocaust, but many historians agree that about six million Jews were killed. Most of them died in the camps.

Three main types of camps developed: **concentration camps, labor camps,** and **death camps.** They were run by the **SS,** a special military unit of Nazi elite that swore loyalty to Hitler, rather than Germany. This book will show what life was like for prisoners in the camps.

Surviving the Camps

Millions of people died in the camps, but some survived. The women and children here were **liberated** from Auschwitz camp after the war. They were especially lucky to survive. The Nazis saw women and children as less useful because they were not as strong as men. They often killed the women and children right away.

GREAT BRITAIN

DENMARK

SWEDEN

SOVIET UNION

HOLLAND

BELGIUM

FRANCE

GERMANY

AUSTRIA

SLOVAKIA

POLAND

Neuengamme ○
Ludwigslust ●
Treglitz ●
Ravensbrück ○
Bergen-Belsen ○
Hannover ●
Braunschweig ●
Sachsenhausen ○
Weihagen ●
Nordhausen ●
Dora ●
Krawinkel ●
Flössberg ●
Buchenwald ○
Rehmsdorf ●
Dresden ●
Bautzen ●
Ohrdruf ○
Gross Rosen ○
Sonneburg ●
Terezín ○
Flossenbürg ○
Hessenthal ●
Natzweiler ○
Spaichingen ●
Buchenwald ○
Dachau ○
Gusen ○
Mauthausen ○
Gunskirchen ○

Stutthof ○
Lieberose ●
Schlieben ○
Otoczno ○
Chelmo ●
Treblinka ●
Koluszki ○
Skarzysko-Kamienna
Piotrkow ○
Blizyn ○
Deblin ○
Poniatowa ○
Sobibor ●
Lublin ○
Izbica ○
Trawniki ○
Starachowice ○
Zawiercie ○
Majdanek ●
Gliwice ○
Sosnowiec ○
Budzyn ○
Katowice ○
Auschwitz ●
Mielec ○
Belzec ●
Monowitz ●
Plaszow ○
Pustkow ○
Rzeszow ○
Szebnie ○

● **Death camps**
● **Combined camps**
○ **Concentration camps**
○ **Labor camps in Poland**
● **Labor camps in Germany**

Camps in Greater Germany

This map shows the death camps and the biggest concentration camps and labor camps set up by the Nazis in **Greater Germany.** It does not show the smaller labor and concentration camps, or the many sub-camps that grew around the big camps. Nor does this map show camps in other parts of German-**occupied** Europe.

How Do We Know?

- One of the most important sources of information comes from people who survived the camps. Camp prisoners are the only people who know exactly what life was like. Some told their memories directly. Others wrote stories and poems, or painted and drew the camps.
- Some who did not survive hid writings or pictures that were later found.
- There are official Nazi documents that show what went on in the camps. They only give the Nazi view of camp life. At the end of the war, the Nazis tried to destroy the evidence of what went on in the camps, but many records and photos have survived.
- Many camps, such as Mauthausen and Auschwitz-Birkenau, still stand.
- After the war some Nazis, especially many who had been in the SS, were imprisoned and tried for war crimes. The trials heard evidence from survivors, members of the SS, and people who worked for the SS in the camps.
- The soldiers who liberated the camps recorded what they were like in words, on film, and in pictures.

The Camps

There were several types of camps, and the system was expanded and changed over time. The people who were imprisoned changed, and so did the **Nazis'** reasons for imprisoning them. Some things did not change. The camps were always run by the **SS**—short for *Schutzstaffel* or "security staff"—a military unit that began as Hitler's special bodyguard. People were always sent to the camps without trial and for as long as the SS wanted them there. Conditions in the camps were always brutal.

Who Was Sent to the Camps?

Between 1933 and 1935, **political** opponents of the Nazis were the most likely to be sent to the camps. At first, the Nazis focused on **Communists.** The camps, and the laws allowing the police to send people to the camps without trial, were set up after the *Reichstag* (the German Parliament) burned down in 1933. The Nazis made it seem as if Communists had started the fire. Very soon, however, the Nazis started arresting leaders and members of any other political parties or trade unions as "political" opponents of the Nazi party.

Types of Camps

- **Concentration camps** were the first Nazi camps. The Nazis said concentration camp prisoners would be "re-educated" to accept Nazi beliefs through "exercise, discipline, and hard work," and then released. Some were, but many were not.

- The Nazis also set up **labor camps** near factories or workplaces, such as stone quarries, to provide cheap workers. Even in labor camps, work was never the main concern. The most important concern of the camp was to work prisoners to death. As the war went on, both the concentration camps and labor camps set up smaller sub-camps near factories, quarries, and mines.

- **Death camps** were set up from 1941 on to kill as many **Jews** as possible, as efficiently as possible. Four new camps were built as death camps: Chelmno, Belzec, Sobibor, and Treblinka. Death camps were also added to two existing camps, Majdanek and Auschwitz.

No More Camps?

By 1935, most political opposition to the Nazis was either crushed or so secret that few opponents were caught. The Nazis considered closing the camps—there were just 3,000 prisoners left in them, the lowest number since they were first set up. Hitler and the other Nazi leaders decided to expand the camps system instead. They began to fill the camps with different kinds of people, all of whom the Nazis saw as **"undesirable."**

Asocials

Asocials were people who the Nazis saw as failing in their duty to the state. This group included people who refused to work, bums, drunks, gamblers, petty criminals, people who fell into debt, and people who were seen as not bringing up their children properly. It also included homosexuals and people from groups that refused to swear an oath of loyalty to Hitler, such as **Jehovah's Witnesses.**

Transit Camps

From 1938 onward, Germany began to take control, usually by force, of other European countries. Jews and non-Aryans from these countries were sent to the camps. Transit camps, like this one in Drancy, France, were set up in **occupied** countries such as France, Holland, and Belgium. Millions of people were held in these camps until they could be taken to camps in Germany, Czechoslovakia, or Poland—countries under German control.

Racial Inferiors

The Nazis had complicated, entirely invented ideas about **race.** The Nazis wanted to fill the **Third Reich** with "pure" Germans, who they saw as belonging to an invented race called **Aryan.** The other western European groups were beneath the Aryans. More inferior were eastern and southern European peoples, Asian and African peoples, then Slavs and Gypsies, and, worst of all to the Nazis, Jews.

Running the Camps

The **SS** ran the camps. Although they were a military unit, they reported directly to the SS commander, Heinrich Himmler. Himmler reported directly to Hitler. Each camp, however small, had a camp **commandant** and some guards. In between the commandant and guards came a varying number of SS officers who organized supplies and equipment, as well as other aspects of camp life such as hiring prisoners out as workers.

Kapos

The camps were organized so that some prisoners, called **kapos,** did the actual day-to-day supervision of other prisoners. *Kapos* were usually criminals, preferably German criminals.

Kapos reported to the SS and were given privileges for working for the SS. *Kapos* in charge of work groups did not have to do any of the hard, difficult work themselves. They had the power to punish, even murder, other prisoners. However, they were like all of the other prisoners—entirely at the mercy of the SS and could lose their job at any time. Ana Novac remembers the **blockälteste** in charge of her barracks:

> *Felicie is in charge of our barracks. Her "place in the sun" gets her quite a bit of extra bread and jam but makes her very tense, nervous. She arrives two hours before each **roll call,** counts and recounts us 25 times, and yet she still gets it wrong. So the Germans slap her, in front of us, and she slaps us in return.*

Meeting at Roll Call

At roll call each day, the camp commandant met with some of his officers and looked over the prisoners. In this photo, the camp commandant (with his back to us) is being given the daily report on the number of prisoners who had died that day.

Female *Kapos*

The women's camps had female *kapos*. They dressed like the other prisoners, although their clothes were usually more suited to the weather—they had coats in winter, for example. In this picture of the weaving shed at Ravensbrück camp in Germany, the women with headscarves are ordinary prisoners. The woman on the left of the aisle with a long dark coat and a cap is probably a *kapo*.

Constant Fear

The SS did not want revolts or escape attempts in the camps. Thus, they worked hard to stop prisoners from making friends and meeting in groups. They promised extra rations or better work to people who informed on other prisoners. They made punishments very harsh to increase the atmosphere of fear and terror. Prisoners could be hanged for a minor offense, such as meeting in a group. The SS changed work gangs and moved people from camp to camp. All of this, added to the hundreds of deaths every day, made it hard for prisoners to form trustworthy groups.

Different Camp Experiences

A prisoner's camp life varied depending on many factors.

- The year: In the early 1930s, when the camps were mainly used to imprison **political** opponents, it was possible to be released from them. Even **Jewish** prisoners were released. Many of them were convinced by their camp experiences to leave Germany.

- The camp: The type of camp people were sent to was important. Small **labor camps** could be less brutal than bigger camps, such as Auschwitz. **Death camps** were different. People, mostly Jews, were sent to them to be killed.

- The guards: What life was like also depended on who was in charge of your daily routine. Some guards were more brutal than others.

- The prisoners: A prisoner's **race** affected his or her camp experience. German criminals, who the SS used as *kapos*, had a very different life than Jewish prisoners, who were the least important.

Processing Arrivals

As soon as they arrived in the camps, prisoners were no longer seen as people. They went through a step-by-step process, intended to strip away everything that made them human individuals. Even though many of them had already been in prison and been badly treated by the **Gestapo,** most new prisoners were not prepared for the indignity of arriving at their first camp.

The Same System

In almost all of the camps, the arrival process was the same for new prisoners and prisoners being transferred from other camps.

- Prisoners were made to undress.
- All of the prisoners' hair was shaved.
- They had to shower and be disinfected.
- They were given uniforms and a camp number.
- Finally, the prisoners were herded off to barracks. All new prisoners, and some who were moved from other camps, then spent several days in **"quarantine,"** cut off from the rest of the camp until they learned camp routine.

Mieczyslaw Karczewski remembers arriving at Mauthausen:

*The first shock was when this **SS** guy comes up and he says, take off your clothes. I thought, where? You mean here? It was raining; we were weak from a long **transport,** hungry, too. They had made us stand for hours at some wall and now they were expecting us to take our clothes off. We stood there naked in the snow and rain. . . . Then we were given a number and off to the barracks.*

Dogs

New arrivals in Mauthausen camp were met by SS guards with dogs trained to attack prisoners. Leon Zelman, a **political** prisoner who survived the camp, remembers how the dogs were used to terrorize prisoners on a daily basis:

The SS men and their dogs were behind us every day as we came back from work. If anyone collapsed they were there right away, the dogs attacking and barking ferociously. Anyone who did not get back on their feet after this was shot in the neck.

Arriving in Mauthausen

Arrivals at Mauthausen were processed in the large central square. This area was also used for **roll call** and disinfection, large scale hosing down with chemicals to kill lice.

Fear and Uncertainty

While the process of dealing with new arrivals was usually the same from camp to camp, the SS made sure that there were enough differences to keep the prisoners terrified and uncertain. Sometimes they unloaded trains or trucks at once and made the new arrivals rush through the processing routine "at the double"— running. Other times they made the process last all day, with the prisoners standing around, often naked, in snow, rain, or baking heat. Survivors remember the fear and uncertainty at every stage, and the certainty that the SS would beat people to death or shoot them for any reason, real or imagined.

Less Than Human

The camp system tried to take away prisoners' individuality during the arrival process. From then on, the system was designed to continue to treat people as if they were less than human to underline how little their lives were worth.

Tadeusz Sobolewicz remembers arriving at Auschwitz camp, aged seventeen, puzzled by the brutality of the SS, and even more so by that of the ***kapos:***

> *All the time I was asking myself: "Why are they beating us so? Why?" The* kapos *were prisoners like us yet they beat us so eagerly, as if we were their enemies. . . . Why didn't anyone explain what we should do, instead of hitting us first?*

The SS and the *kapos* used prisoners' camp numbers, not their names. Prisoners worked and lived as part of a barrack or work group, not as individuals. When the arrival process was over, it was hard for family and friends to recognize each other—everyone looked the same. This dehumanizing treatment made it easier for the SS to control and mistreat prisoners, because they did not see them as people.

11

The Purpose of Quarantine

New arrivals were sent to **quarantine.** It was supposed to be a medical quarantine, to make sure the new arrivals did not have any diseases that could spread to the rest of the camp. In fact, quarantine was to terrorize the new arrivals so that, when they joined the rest of the camp, they would be obedient and work hard. Roman Frister, a Polish **Jew** who survived four different camps, said: "The **Nazis** surrounded us not only with barbed wire, but also with a wall of orders and rules that demanded blind obedience."

Quarantine Barracks

This is a photograph of the quarantine barracks in Auschwitz-Birkenau camp. They looked just like the other barracks, but were separated by a fence. The quarantine prisoners were not allowed to mix with other prisoners.

Herr Kahn was arrested in 1938 and sent to Buchenwald camp, where he and the rest of the men arrested at the same time spent two days and three nights in quarantine:

There were about 6,000 of us crowded into one barracks which didn't have a floor yet, it was just damp clay. We had bare planks for beds, no mattresses, no blankets, no light. The toilets were disgusting. In the middle of the first night, when things had quieted down a little, we were suddenly blinded by flashlights and about a dozen men were dragged away by the **SS.** *We heard them screaming horribly outside and they never came back. The same thing happened the next two nights. On the third morning we were lined up in front of the barracks. . . . Everyone with a visible injury was asked how it happened. The first few answered truthfully, saying the SS had whipped them. The guards then whipped them over and over until they said they had done it themselves. Then we were led away to new barracks, where conditions were a little better.*

Waiting for Death

This group of Jewish people was transported to Auschwitz-Birkenau death camp from Hungary. The SS photographed them as they waited to be gassed. The SS had told them that they would have a shower and then move on to be resettled the next day.

Arriving in Treblinka

Treblinka was a **death camp.** Prisoners sent to Treblinka were gassed as soon as possible after their arrival, usually within two hours. A hundred or so *Arbeitsjuden*—"work Jews," were kept alive to keep the camp running. They maintained the SS barracks, processed the possessions of the new arrivals, and disposed of the bodies of the dead.

Willi Mentz was an SS man who worked in Treblinka. His job was to shoot the sick and frail people on the **transports.** They were taken off to the so-called hospital area, where they were shot. Presumably, it reassured the prisoners if they thought the sick were getting special care.

Mentz described the arrival and processing at Treblinka:

*When the Jews got out of the wagons they were told they were a **resettlement** transport, that they would be given a shower and new clothes and taken on to where they would live the next day. The women undressed in huts, the men out in the open. The women and children were led down a passageway called "the tube" to the **gas chambers. . . .** There were always ill and frail people on the wagons, as well as dead people. The bodies were unloaded and the sick and frail were brought to the hospital. They were collected up by an open grave and I shot them in the neck. Sometimes there were only two or three, sometimes twenty or more—men, women, and children.*

Friends and Societies

The **SS** tried hard to stop prisoners in the camps from setting up any kind of group or even from making friends. Societies, such as groups of people with the same religious beliefs, could help each other. Groups could plot revolts or escapes, and friends could help keep each other from giving up.

Breaking Up Families

The first thing the SS did was to break up family groups. They divided up the camps by sex—women and young children in one place, men and older boys in another. Family members did still try to stay together, and some managed it. At the age of seventeen, Hugo Gryn was sent to Auschwitz with his father and uncle. They managed to stay together, even moving from camp to camp, but they did not all survive the brutal conditions. Hugo's uncle died in Lieberose sub-camp. His father died in Gunskirchen camp, a few days after the **Allies** reached the camp at the end of the war in 1945.

Selection at Auschwitz

Selections were often made as soon as a train arrived at Auschwitz. The SS sent the old, the young, the sick, and many of the women to the left, and healthy men and boys and some of the women to the right. This photo shows women and children who were sent to their deaths at Auschwitz-Birkenau camp.

Elie Wiesel remembers how his family was divided:

An SS officer came to meet us, a truncheon [club] in his hand. He gave the order: "Men to the left! Women to the right!" Eight words spoken quietly, without emotion. Eight short, simple words. Yet that was the moment when I parted from my mother. I had not had time to think, but already I felt the pressure of my father's hand: we were alone. For a part of a second I glimpsed my mother and my sisters moving away to the right. Tzipora held Mother's hand. I saw them disappear into the distance; my mother was stroking my sister's fair hair, as though to protect her, while I walked on with my father and the other men.

Family Support

Whole families could not stay together, but if those of the same sex could do so, it helped them to keep going. They had emotional support and a practical advantage. They could deal with camp life as a team—they could trust each other. Trust was much harder for strangers meeting for the first time at the camps.

Ana Novac, who was alone when she arrived in Plaszow camp, remembers the three Falk sisters:

> *Each one had her job. Ruchi, the oldest and strongest, was the boss. Feigele's job was to show her dimples, act innocent, try to charm extra food or a soft job out of the* **kapos.** *Surele did whatever else was needed. She was a weak and growing child if there was something left at the bottom of the soup pot. She was sick if she didn't want to work in bad weather. She was strong as an ox if there was a paid job going. Needless to say they managed to get the job of giving out the food for the barracks.*

Gerda Weissmann, a seventeen-year-old Polish girl, and her sister, Ilse, were sent from Bielitz to Bolkenhain camp in June of 1942. They managed to stay together through six changes of camp, all of them small sub-camps. Ilse died on the "death march" into Germany ahead of the advancing Allied armies: "'Promise me one thing,' she said. 'You must try to keep going for one more week.' I did not answer. 'One more week, promise,' she persisted. 'I promise.'" Gerda kept her promise. On the fourth day she was **liberated.**

Making Friends

Many people formed friendships on the **transports** and in the camps, and some people ran into friends from their old lives in the camps. Ana Novac met an old friend in Auschwitz-Birkenau:

> *I was suddenly lifted off my feet, hugged, and there was my old friend Edith, beaming at me. She was a camp cook. She took off her uniform dress (she was wearing another one under it) and I put it on, there, out in the open. She then ran off and came back with a steaming bowl—meat and potatoes all from the bottom of the soup pot.*

Keeping Friends

Friendships made things easier, but they could be broken up by the **SS** moving people around, or by death. Also, the camps affected different people in different ways— they could change people dramatically.

Fania Fénelon, a French singer, met a woman named Clara on the train from Drancy transit camp in France to Auschwitz. They shared their food and promised to stick together. When Fania was chosen for the camp orchestra, she refused to join without Clara. Being in the orchestra gave them much better living conditions than the ordinary prisoners.

Clara found even these better conditions hard to cope with. She refused to share food and then began to suspect the others of taking her food. She cut herself off from them. Then, Clara was made a **kapo:**

> *She stood in front of our little group and pushed her club under our noses. "From now on, I'm the boss. I'm in charge and you do as I say or I'll hit you!" Drunk with noise and violence she lashed out at the weakest and strutted about, claiming to the SS that her block was the most efficient.*

Musical Society

Fania Fénelon was in the women's orchestra at Auschwitz-Birkenau. Several camps had orchestras. The orchestras played marching tunes as prisoners went to and from work each day. They also played concerts for the SS. They were, unusually, a society set up by the SS. This photo, taken by the SS, shows the men's orchestra at Auschwitz I.

Taking Chances

There were people in the camps who took the chance to help anyone they could, as this picture drawn by a survivor shows.

People who worked in the kitchens sometimes managed to smuggle out some extra food. They often took this food to the hospital. Patients in the hospital were given what the SS called "lazy rations," or less food, because they were not working. They had less nourishment just when they needed it most. A bowl of soup, even camp soup, could make the difference between living and dying.

Keeping to Themselves

There were times when even a person's closest friends could not help him or her. Lucie Adelsberger, a **Jewish** doctor in Auschwitz, remembers that it was a rule among the prisoners, as well as an official SS rule, that you did not act to help a friend or family member who was being mistreated. It never helped. Neither the SS nor the *kapos* would listen to a prisoner asking them to spare another prisoner. Lucie Adelsberger remembers one such incident:

> During **roll call** the whole block had to kneel in the snow because the prisoners *who worked in the weaving mill had failed, by only a few meters* [yards]*, to make enough cloth in the day. A girl, weak with fever, fell over, and the* kapos *began beating her. The girl's mother protested. The* kapos *responded by kicking and beating the daughter even harder, and they beat up the mother as well, for her protests.*

Horrors like this made many people decide that the best way to survive in the camps was not to have any friends. They found it easier to cut off their emotions entirely. They focused on keeping themselves alive.

Other Supports

Some people learned to cope with life in the camp by hating the **SS** and wanting to defeat them by surviving. Others were kept going by a sense of humor or the determination to survive. There were also organized activities that kept people from giving up. Some were secret from the **Nazis,** others were not.

Prisoners organized soccer games and other entertainment on Sunday afternoons. Sometimes these were organized by *kapos.* One *kapo* at Mauthausen, Franz Unek, even had wooden cups made to present to the winning team. Stanislaw Gorondowski, a prisoner in Mauthausen, remembers:

> *There were football* [soccer] *games, boxing matches, drama and circus shows organized by the prisoners. And one must not forget the orchestras. All this was a huge contrast to SS brutality, yet they let it happen, they seemed somehow impressed by these shows.*

Music

Some camps had orchestras. The SS had to approve an orchestra before it could be set up. In several camps, including Auschwitz, the SS set up an orchestra. There were several reasons to do so. One was to provide marching music to get everyone to and from work. Another was to show the outside world that camps were not so bad. Even new arrivals were encouraged and asked themselves: "How bad could this camp be if there is an orchestra here?" Finally, the SS could order a camp orchestra to give concerts of the SS's favorite music at any time.

The French singer, Fania Fénelon, remembers that she was grateful for being in the orchestra because it kept her alive. She also felt angry at having to play for the SS and guilty when she played to the other prisoners and saw how much worse their conditions were than her own.

For the Children

The women of Auschwitz-Birkenau's women's camp decorated the walls of the barracks. They painted pictures from traditional fairy tales for the children who lived there.

Secret Radios

Some factory workers stole parts to make secret radios like this one. They could then listen to the news and religious services on the radio.

Religious Beliefs

Many camp prisoners were comforted by their religious beliefs. Religious services were banned, but people did manage to hold services sometimes. For example, on Sunday, November 16, 1941, Konrad Szweda, a Catholic priest, held a secret mass in Block 4 in Auschwitz I camp. The mass was as short as possible and held in a dark, cramped aisle between the bunk beds. If they had been caught, everyone at the mass would have been executed.

Hugo Gryn, who was sent to his first camp at just seventeen, and his fellow **Jews** in Block 4 in Lieberose camp decided to celebrate the Jewish festival of Hanukkah. It fell in the first week of December in 1944. They decided to light a **menorah** every night.

They made the *menorah* with pieces of metal and wood. They saved their margarine to make candles. They made candle wicks out of twisted threads from the edges of their caps. Finally, the first night of Hanukkah arrived and they met to light the *menorah*. Several Catholics and Protestants, even the **blockältester** himself, came, too. They chanted the prayers. Hugo, the youngest one there, tried to light the candles. But the candles would not light because margarine does not burn. Hugo complained to his father about wasting the margarine. He remembers his father's reply:

Patiently he taught me one of the most lasting lessons of my life and I believe that he made my survival possible. "Don't be so angry," he said to me, "you know that this festival celebrates the victory of the spirit over tyranny and might. You and I have had to go once for over a week without proper food and another time almost three days without water, but you cannot live for three minutes without hope."

Living Conditions

Living conditions varied from camp to camp. In the bigger camps, conditions were often harder—there was less space, the food was worse, and the discipline was harsher. Conditions were never good anywhere, but there were camps where the conditions were bearable. When Ana Novac, a young Hungarian girl, was in Auschwitz-Birkenau, she shared a single sleeping space with four other women. When she was transferred to a small **labor camp** at Wiesau, she was amazed by the difference:

> *We are told we will wash daily, that there will be hot water to wash in. There are four or five rooms to each barracks, twenty bunks to a room and one person to a bunk. One! With a blanket! A pillow! A spoon and a real plate! The soup is real, proper soup, too, and the bread is fresh.*

These conditions were unusually good.

Housing

In most camps the prisoners lived in barracks. Where there was overcrowding, or where the prisoners were building a new camp, they lived in tents. Wherever they were, the prisoners were crowded together. They either slept on the floor—if they were lucky they got straw or straw mattresses to sleep on—or in bunks. If they slept in bunks, it was usually several prisoners to a bunk. In these conditions, diseases, lice, and fleas spread rapidly. Ana Novac remembers conditions in Auschwitz-Birkenau:

Sleeping Places

These photos show the bunks in Auschwitz I (top) and the sleeping shelves in Auschwitz-Birkenau (bottom). People usually slept three or four to a bunk, with straw mattresses. The sleeping shelves usually had eight to ten people in them.

*They say a **transport** of Italian women are to be moved into our barracks. They turn out to be Greeks, from Rhodes. What difference, anyway? It is 300 more to argue over blankets and space. Now you can only all turn over together. . . . It's impossible to sleep on your back—even raising my knees a little causes grumbling from all sides.*

Sanitation

Camp barracks, toilets, and washrooms were painted with sayings like: "Cleanliness is your duty." Despite these messages, camp **sanitation** was so bad that it was impossible for prisoners to stay clean. Prisoners often had only a few wells or a tap or two outside for washing, and a huge toilet pit. Even with toilets and washrooms, prisoners were not allowed to use them sensibly. They had a minute or so to wash in the mornings and a similar amount of time to use the toilets. They were not allowed to leave the barracks at night. Rarely they were given a toilet bucket to use in the barracks.

Disinfection

The **SS** regularly disinfected prisoners. They made this as unpleasant as possible—prisoners had to wait while naked. Sometimes they had to run around the nearest square, or do exercises. A few prisoners died during each disinfection. Tadeusz Sobolewicz remembers:

> It took three hours for us to get to the vat. We had been naked all the time. . . . When we got there they were dragging a body out of the tub. There were already four corpses stacked against the wall. I quickly climbed into the tub. The water was freezing, but it also burned me—there was clearly too much chlorine in the tub. But I went right under—before they could push me under and hold me there.

Washrooms and Toilets

These photos show the washroom and toilets in Auschwitz I. When the camps were in use, they would have been full of people desperate to use them. Prisoners were only allowed into them for a short time first thing in the morning.

Three Meals a Day

Camp prisoners were given three meals a day: breakfast, a meal some time after noon, and a meal in the evening. The **SS** set down rules for what these meals were to be.

The menus were based on providing the least amount of food necessary to keep people alive and working. Non-working prisoners, such as those in the hospital, were given less. The average breakfast was only 15 ounces (500 ml) of coffee or tea. Lunch was less than a quart (750 ml) of soup, with meat four times a week. The evening meal was 2/3 pound (300 g) of bread, an ounce (25 g) of margarine, an ounce (25 g) of sausage or cheese, and a spoonful of jam. Prisoners seldom got even this.

Desperate for Food

This picture was painted by a camp prisoner after the camps had been **liberated.** It shows how the prisoners were so desperate for food that they would even scoop up the disgusting "camp soup" from the ground to eat it.

The Quality of Food

The food provided was tested from time to time by the SS Hygienic Institute, which created the menus in the first place. A report carried out by Dr. Hans Munch noted that the soup served in Auschwitz I was regularly missing well over half the fat it should have had. The prisoners' sausage had half the fat of the sausage eaten by the SS, despite the fact that they were both made in the same place and were supposed to be made from the same recipe. Coffee and tea were made from ground up acorns or birch leaves. The soup, bread, and jam often included sawdust and other, less edible things, such as sand or pebbles.

Food Packages

The camp rules said that prisoners could be sent food packages. In 1943, the **Red Cross** began to send packages, too. They had to be addressed to people by name, giving the camp name and the prisoner's camp number. It was hard for the Red Cross

to get this information, so many packages were sent straight to the SS or the camp kitchens. Even properly addressed packages did not always make it to the person they were sent to.

Packages were checked by the SS—for weapons and so on, supposedly. While checking, the SS took whatever they wanted. In 1944, camp **commandants** were told that all packages from outside **Greater Germany,** from people or organizations, were to be sent to the camp kitchens, even if they were properly addressed.

Too Weak to Eat

Constant underfeeding left many prisoners too weak to eat when they were liberated. These prisoners at Ebensee camp were given sugar cubes to suck to keep their strength up.

"Cooking With the Mouth"

In all the camps, big or small, people were starving. Yet many prisoners, men and women, talked about food. Some even wrote down recipes. Gerda Weissmann, who was first sent to the camps as a teenager, remembers:

> *In Helmbrechts, a small camp of perhaps a dozen barracks, we were all sick. We had very little food because we were not working anymore . . . many of the girls began talking about food. They started to swap recipes for*

> *the richest pastries and cakes they could think of. I found it terrible to listen to, it made my hunger worse.*

Susan E. Cernyak-Spatz, who had been a prisoner in Auschwitz and Terezín, says:

> *There was a camp expression for all the talk of food. We called it "cooking with the mouth." Everybody did it. And people got very upset if they thought you made a dish the wrong way, or used the wrong ingredients.*

Illness

Everyone got sick in the camps. The crowded conditions, dreadful **sanitation,** and poor food meant that diseases, especially dysentery and **typhus,** spread quickly and hit almost everyone. **TB** and other lung diseases also spread quickly. Prisoners soon realized that, for several reasons, they had to hide their sickness for as long as they could.

Less Food

Often people in the hospital were put on "lazy rations"—smaller portions of food—because they were not working. Even if food was sent to the hospital, the patients often did not get to eat it. Patients who were sent to act as nurses often kept the food for themselves. When they did give food to the patients, many were too sick to eat it or too weak to feed themselves.

Inadequate Treatment

The sick did not get proper medical treatment in the hospitals. They were dumped there to get better by themselves or die. Some camps allowed prisoners who were doctors to work in the hospitals and give the prisoners some care. They very seldom gave them any medicine for the patients, though. In other camps, doctors and other patients had to look after the sick secretly. Doctors, while not expected to care for the sick, were expected to fill out detailed forms on each patient every day. They also had to make sure that they had the right number of patients there—otherwise they would be beaten.

Experiments

These are some of the drugs that the **SS** tested on prisoners for the company I.G. Farben. The drugs often had horrific side effects and were not made for general use. The sick in the hospitals were guinea pigs for these drugs. Drug testing only went on in the larger camps, where SS doctors had many **Jewish** people on hand to use in their experiments. The prisoners experimented on were mainly Jewish because the Nazis saw them as the most worthless.

"Raspberry Picking"

In Mauthausen, the sick were often given a tin cup and told that they were going to do "light work" picking berries. While being marched along, they were shot by the SS—supposedly while "trying to escape"—like the prisoner shown here. The SS liked these "raspberry picking details" because guards who shot prisoners trying to escape were often given time off in reward.

No Value

The sick could not work, so the SS saw them as a drain on the camp. That is why they did not provide the hospitals with anything they needed to care for the sick. Erwin Gostner, a prisoner who survived Mauthausen, remembers:

> The sick lie on straw bags and are left there, with no care, until they are dead. Then they are stacked up in the washroom for the daily collection. . . . New patients are stacked straight on to the straw bags the dead have left, which are smeared with blood and filth.

Killed Off

If the sick did not die quickly enough, they were "helped." In Mauthausen this "help" included long **roll calls** outside in their underwear or cold showers out in the open. The SS also held **selections** of the sickest almost daily. The selected prisoners were killed at once. The selections were made by SS doctors. The selected patients were killed in various ways. They could be left without food or water, to starve, but this was slow and did not free a bed for the next sick person. Instead, the SS hurried their deaths along. The doctors might kill them by injecting a drug, usually phenol, which gave them a heart attack. Otherwise, the SS gassed or shot them.

Discipline

The camps had a strict set of rules and a harsh system of punishments. They were worked out for Dachau camp, the first camp set up. They were later applied to all camps. While the official rules and punishments were hard, actual camp life was harder. In reality, the **SS** could punish prisoners for anything or nothing, and they could make up any punishments they wanted. *Kapos* and other **prisoner functionaries** were encouraged to make up cruel punishments, especially for **Jewish** prisoners.

Learning the Rules

Often, prisoners were not told the rules; they had to figure them out for themselves. This added to the atmosphere of fear and uncertainty in the camp.

Ana Novac remembers one incident in Auschwitz-Birkenau:

*We had a shock this morning. The new arrivals have cut up several blankets to wrap around themselves! "It's cold," they explain to Solange, the speechless kapo. So now they have to stay on their knees during **roll call** for the next four days and have no food at all for two. At roll call, the SS in charge whips them without mercy.*

Punishments

Groups of prisoners were often punished by day-long roll calls. At these roll calls prisoners had to stand at attention, remove and replace their caps, and do various other things all day. The prisoners had no food or drink. If they did anything wrong, they were beaten, sometimes to death. Some people died from exhaustion. Individual prisoners could be punished by beatings or whipping. They could be hanged from beams or made to kneel on piles of sharp stones for hours. They could be sent to the camp prison to be locked in the cells or sent to the punishment unit— a special barracks where they had to work harder for longer and were given less food. Prisoners sent to the punishment unit were not expected to survive.

A Beating

This photo shows an SS guard beating a prisoner at Poniatowa camp in Poland. Beatings took place every day.

Missing Roll Call

It was serious for the SS when a prisoner was not at roll call. It meant the prisoner may have escaped. Camp rules did not say that missing roll call was punishable by death, but in many camps this was what happened. Sometimes prisoners were sent to the punishment unit that worked prisoners to death. Other times they were simply beaten to death in front of the other prisoners. Ana Novac remembers this in Plaszow camp:

> *The count was off. There was one missing. They counted over and over. She was found in the barracks, asleep. She was taken out to the roll call square. . . . It went dead quiet, as if everyone there had stopped breathing all at once. We knew she was lost.*

> *She hadn't realized yet, she was new. . . . He ordered her to undress, then carefully took off his leather jacket and folded it, putting it on the ground well out of the way. This careful preparation for murder upset me more than what followed. He beat her to death. Luckily, she fainted almost at once.*

Roll Call

This painting of roll call in Auschwitz I on a Christmas Eve was painted by a camp prisoner after the camps were **liberated** and the war was over. You can see a *kapo* hitting a prisoner and an SS officer adding up the counts in his book. You can also see the pile of people who have already died at this roll call. In the block of prisoners on the left, at the front of the picture, you can see another person who has died and has not yet been moved to the pile.

Work

All prisoners in every kind of camp had to work unless they were sick. Because the sick were simply sent to the hospital to die, people worked on for as long as they could. Eventually, the prisoners became a vital part of **Nazi** war production. More and more often, camps and sub-camps were built with factories or near existing factories.

However, work had another purpose. The camps were expected to work people to death. It was the Nazi idea of *Vernichtung durch Arbeit* or "destruction through work." From the start, work of all kinds, in all camps, was expected to kill all but the strongest within months or even weeks. Every job was made as difficult and dangerous as possible. Had the Nazis wanted their prisoners to work efficiently, they would have provided basic tools, such as wheelbarrows for moving heavy loads.

Arbeit Macht Frei

These are the gates of Auschwitz I. Several camp gates had *Arbeit Macht Frei*—"Work will set you free"—written on them. It sounds as if the Nazis were saying: "If you work hard and learn your lesson, you will be allowed to go home." This was not the message at all, however. Work only set Nazi prisoners free by killing them. Karl Fritzsch, *Schutzhaftlagerfürher* (camp **commandant**) at Auschwitz I, made the same speech to all prisoners when they arrived, telling them what to expect:

This is not a sanatarium [health resort] but a German **concentration camp.** *There is only one exit: through the* **crematorium** *chimney.* **Jews** *may live for two weeks, priests for one month, the rest for three months. Anyone who does not like what I say can throw himself on the electric fence. That, too, is a way out.*

Oranienburg

This photo shows political prisoners in Oranienburg camp in 1933, shortly after the Nazis came to power. The camp was later rebuilt at nearby Sachsenhausen. The photo was taken to suggest that the camps kept people reasonably well fed and dressed and worked them, but not too hard.

Building the Camps

The first camp prisoners often had to build the camp. They lived in tents or old buildings already on the site until they built the barracks. Once the camps were built, prisoners kept them running. They worked in the kitchens, offices, hospitals, and stores. They also cleaned the camp, dug ditches, and built additions to the camp.

Depending on where the camp was built, the prisoners were also sent to work in nearby factories, mines, steelworks, or quarries. The **SS,** who ran the camps, made a profit from hiring out their prisoners.

Different Kinds of Work

Different prisoners did different work—the SS made clear distinctions among them. Criminals, especially German criminals, got the easy jobs and could become **kapos.** Jews and other groups seen by the Nazis as **racially** inferior got the worst jobs. Tadeusz Sobolewicz, a Polish **political** prisoner, remembers:

We had to unload sacks of cement. They were heavy, but manageable. But the SS made us move them running, "at the double," beaten for every act of "sabotage," such as letting a sack fall.

Dangerous Jobs

The SS could turn almost any job into a dangerous one. Kitchen work was seen as a good job, but every day about twenty prisoners died while moving boxes of potatoes to the kitchens at Auschwitz I. They died because the SS made their job impossible.

Two prisoners carried each box, which weighed more than two fit men could carry. If they fell, the box crushed them, or they were clubbed to death for dropping it. If they stayed on their feet they were still likely to drop the box, and be killed for doing so.

Skilled Workers?

Camp prisoners soon saw that it was important to keep working. Working, especially in factories or other places that paid the **SS,** made them useful and so more likely to live. Factories preferred workers with useful skills. When the SS asked at **roll call** for carpenters, lathe operators, or cloth makers, prisoners volunteered, even if they did not have these skills. Hugo Gryn told the SS he was a carpenter. At Lieberose camp, Hugo was told to:

> *"Oil those saws and then start cutting wood for tables and chairs. The designs and measurements are on that sheet." The oiling part was easy. I was made for oiling saws, I thought. But the chairs and tables—how was I going to cut those to measure? Just then an SS man came in and demanded wood for the guard room.*

Hugo cut some wood. The SS man did not tell him to stop, so he cut all the rest—a week's worth of wood. Luckily, the **kapo** thought it was funny and taught Hugo to do the job properly.

Women's Work

Women prisoners were also worked to death, and treated just as badly as the male prisoners. Magda Somogyi worked building roads in 1944:

> *Once I dropped a huge stone because it was so heavy. The SS man whipped me for dropping the stone. From then on, every day he whipped me before work began saying: "Do you understand? You will learn that you do not need to drop the stone." He was right. I didn't drop a stone again.*

Other work that women had to do included digging drainage ditches knee-deep in swamp water and digging out the pits that the block toilets drained into.

Ravensbrück

This is a picture of Ravensbrück camp. Ravensbrück was a women's camp—although men and women were locked in the prison. These prisoners were local **politicals** who were kept there until the **Nazis** could decide which camp to send them to, or whether to execute them there.

More Workers Needed

At first, almost all prisoners were seen as expendable—not important enough to keep alive. As more Germans joined the armed forces, the Nazis ran short of workers to do vital war work. On May 15, 1943, all camp **commandants** were told:

> *The urgency of the work being carried out by prisoners requires that every prisoner work to the highest level. Results must be improved by leading and educating the prisoners and by granting them privileges.*

Privileges included not standing for hours on roll call and not being beaten "unnecessarily." Prisoners could "earn" extra food or tobacco. Privileges were given to prisoners doing the most "technical" jobs. The hardest, most dangerous work had no privileges.

A Conflict of Interests

The SS who were responsible for organizing the work of the camps understood the need for improved living and working conditions for the prisoners who did war work. The SS who ran individual camps often did not; many clung to the idea of "death through work." Both groups seemed to agree, however, that **Jews** were still to be brutally treated, rather than given improved conditions. In Mauthausen camp, for example, the death rate for most prisoners went down once they began doing war work. The death rate for Jews was close to 100 percent all of the time.

31

Mauthausen

On August 8, 1938, prisoners from Dachau camp were sent to the stone quarries of Wiener Graben, near Linz, Germany. They built Mauthausen camp, from stone, with their bare hands and very few tools. At first, the prisoners worked mainly in the quarries. Working hours were from 6:30 A.M. to 6:30 P.M. in the lightest part of the summer. Winter working hours were shorter, but the weather made conditions harder. The prisoners often worked barefoot in ice and snow. Milos Vitek, a Czech survivor from Mauthausen, remembers that just getting to work was an ordeal:

> *As we went down the stairs to the quarry the* Blockführer *began to whip the last five in line. They tried to dodge the blows, so bumped into those in front. So the whole hundred-man unit fell in a tangle to the quarry at the bottom. Because we were not in a line the* **kapos** *then beat us with clubs. At this point we usually lost our wooden clogs, so had to do a day's work barefooted. There were several dead before the day's work even began.*

Digging Stone

Work in the quarries, as shown here, continued all through the war. In the spring of 1943, the **SS** also began to make machine guns, aircraft engines, and whole aircraft at Mauthausen. Prisoners built a set of sub-camps, including armament plants, some of which were underground. From December 1943 to December 1944, skilled workers were given bonus coupons that could be exchanged for food, if there was any, at the camp kitchen. **Jews** and other so-called **racially** inferior groups continued to work in the quarries. Their conditions did not improve.

Building Dora

On August 28, 1943, 107 prisoners were taken in trucks from Buchenwald **concentration camp** to an old mine used by the **Nazis** to store gasoline. They were to be the first of thousands of prisoners working in a secret factory making a new German "wonder weapon"—the V-2 long-range rocket. The camp was named Dora. The prisoners first had to finish the underground factory. Their barracks were left until last. Meanwhile, they slept on straw in the tunnels they were digging. There were no toilets or drains, and the tunnels got very little air. They stank of sewage and poisonous gas from the explosives used to clear the tunnels.

In the first six months, 6,000 prisoners died or were killed because the conditions made them too ill to work.

Building Rockets

By April 1944, Dora was ready. Conditions for the workers improved as they dug and moved into their own barracks. Also, because they were working on war production, the SS rules about improved conditions applied to them. It did not last, however. From November 1944 to April 1945, when the camp was **liberated,** more and more prisoners from other camps were marched ahead of the Russian army to Dora, and conditions worsened.

Death in the Camps

People died in all of the **Nazi** camps, all the time. From the start, the death rate was highest for prisoners the Nazis saw as **racially** inferior—Poles, Russians, and especially **Jews.** Hitler had a fierce hatred for Jewish people that he encouraged everyone in Germany, and the lands taken over by Germany, to share. He wanted to make these places *Judenfrei*—"Jew Free."

At first, the Nazis had tried to make life so difficult for Jewish people that they would leave Germany, but not enough left. Then the Nazis began to herd Jews into the camps, encouraging the **SS** to treat them so badly that they died. As the German army invaded Russia, death squads, called *Einsatzgruppen,* followed. Their job was to kill as many Jews as they could find. Even this did not get rid of the Jews quickly enough for Hitler.

The "Final Solution"

On January 20, 1942, fifteen important Nazi leaders met in Wannsee, near Berlin, to agree on a "Final Solution" to what the Nazis called the "Jewish Problem." Hitler was not there. But Reinhard Heydrich, head of the German Secret Services, who led the meeting and was put in charge of making its decisions work, made it clear the orders came from Hitler.

Heydrich announced that all Jews in lands controlled by Germany were to be killed. It was the job of the SS to find the most efficient way of doing it. This meant killing large numbers of people at once, quickly and cheaply. It also meant finding a way of killing that was not "upsetting" for the SS men who did it.

Einsatzgruppen

The *Einsatzgruppen* shot Russian Jews, one by one, as shown here. They did it as efficiently as possible. They made the Jews dig a mass grave first and killed them right on the edge of it, to cut down on the work the soldiers had to do. Even so, this method of mass murder was not efficient enough for the Nazis. It was too slow, it used too much valuable ammunition (needed for the war), and it upset some of the soldiers who had to do it.

34

Death Camps

The SS had already been secretly experimenting with mass murder. They had decided that some sort of gassing was quickest, cheapest, and least upsetting for the murderers. Four **death camps** were set up: Chelmno, Belzec, Sobibor, and Treblinka. There were also death camps built at the existing camps of Auschwitz and Majdanek.

The officials who ran the camps expected to process each **transport** of Jews within two hours. The camps had few barracks or other buildings—they did not need them. Most of the arrivals did not work, eat, or sleep at these camps. Only a few hundred "work Jews" were left alive to keep things going. The **commandant** of Treblinka camp wrote to the Ministry of Transport on July 28, 1942, saying that the transports were bringing in 5,000 Jews a day.

Auschwitz-Birkenau

Auschwitz-Birkenau was the death camp set up near the existing **concentration** and **labor camps** of Auschwitz. Millions of **"undesirables,"** most of them Jewish, were brought to the camp by train in cattle trucks. The trains brought them in through this entrance and stopped by a long platform. There, the trucks were opened and the people unloaded. Sometimes they were all taken straight to the **gas chambers.** Sometimes some people were selected to live and work for a while. However, everyone sent to Auschwitz-Birkenau was simply waiting for his or her turn to be gassed.

The Killing Process

The Auschwitz State Museum has reconstructed a **gas chamber** at Auschwitz I, to show visitors how the process worked.

1. The people to be gassed were herded, naked, into a large, bare room, supposedly for a shower. Some rooms even had pipes and showerheads to look more convincing.

2. The room had thick walls, and strong locks.

3. Zyklon B crystals, which gave off a poisonous gas, were poured either into the system of pipes and shower heads, or directly into the room, through holes in the ceiling, like the one shown here. Most people died within ten minutes, depending on how close they were to the gas and on how old or sick they were. The SS left the room closed off for 30 minutes, just to be sure that everyone was dead.

4. The bodies were taken out and burned in **crematoria.**

Secrets

In Majdanek and Auschwitz, where **death camps** were attached to existing camps, the **SS** were told to keep the camps a secret. Anyone who stayed in these camps for any amount of time soon either figured out what was going on or was told by another prisoner or a **kapo.** Fania Fenelon asked the *kapo* in charge of her barracks what had happened to the people she had traveled with who had been loaded on to trucks marked with red crosses. At first, the *kapo* did not answer. Fania asked again and the *kapo* dragged her to the door:

> *"Look . . ." She pointed to a low building about 50 yards [46 meters] away, above which rose a chimney. "You see that smoke coming from that chimney over there? That's your friends, cooking." "All of them?" "All of them."*

Sonderkommando

Once people had been gassed, the SS had the problem of disposing of the bodies. It was done by special units of **Jewish** men called *Sonderkommando*. They had to take people into the gas chambers and clear the gas chambers out afterwards. They had to check that no one was left alive and then strip the bodies, removing anything of value from them, such as gold teeth. Then, they had to dispose of the bodies. The dead had not been treated with any respect while they were alive—their bodies were not treated with any respect after death either.

Body Disposal

There were so many bodies, thousands every day, that it was hard to dispose of them all. The SS tried piling the bodies into huge pits and covering them with lime to speed up the decomposition process. The process was still too slow, though, and took up too much space. It also left too much evidence behind. They also tried pouring fuel over the bodies and setting fire to them, but this wasted fuel, which became more and more scarce during the war.

So, the SS burned as many bodies as possible in crematoria. The death camps needed several crematoria, running all the time, to get rid of the bodies. Even then, they had a lot of ash from the bodies to dispose of. The ash was dumped in pits or lakes, or simply piled up to be disposed of later, when the "Final Solution" had been completed and the death camps could be shut down.

Burning Bodies

When Auschwitz-Birkenau was gassing the greatest number of people daily, the five crematoria could not cope with the number of bodies. At this time, or when a crematorium broke down, bodies were loaded into mass graves and burned. This photo was taken secretly by a *Sonderkommando*. He gave it to a Polish **political** prisoner, who managed to smuggle it out of the camp.

Leaving the Camps

Some people were released from the camps. From 1933 to 1935, most prisoners were **"politicals"** and were released when the **Nazis** thought they would no longer be a threat to the Nazi state. Even then, they were watched.

A Released "Political"

Walther P. was released in September 1936 and went to live in Naumberg, Germany. He had to go to the local police station and sign a statement:

> *I hereby submit my certificate of release from Lichtenburg* **concentration camp.** *I must report to the local police, criminal department, room 114, every Wednesday and Saturday at 11 o'clock. I shall do this punctually.*

On April 28, 1937, the Naumberg police sent a report to Berlin:

> *Walther P. has obeyed the police order to appear twice a week. He finds this extremely unpleasant and embarrassing. He has repeatedly asked to be released from it.*

> *P. performs his job regularly and lives quietly. He has no contact with people who are suspected of hostility to the State. P. is a member of the German Labor Front and is obviously trying to be part of the National Community. Further strict observation of P. no longer seems necessary.*

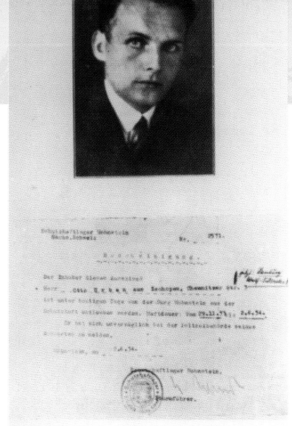

AREA 12 GERMANY TERRORISM;CONCENTRATION CAMPS 1934.- RELEASE CERTIFICATE FROM THE CONCENTRATION CAMP HOHNSTEIN IN SAXONY STATE.

CCS 736311

Released from Hohnstein

This is the release certificate of Otto Urban, who was in prison in Hohnstein camp, in Germany, from November 29, 1933 to June 2, 1934. All release documents had to have an official stamp and the signature of the camp **commandant.**

A Released Jew

Some **Jewish** prisoners were released before war broke out in September 1939. Herr Kahn was released from Buchenwald:

> *We were shaved and our hair cut. An* **SS** *officer said he hoped we were rehabilitated and to prove it we should contribute to* **Winter Aid.** *A collecting box was produced and we all had to give something. We gave in, and paid . . . for*

"tickets" home. No one could leave until all had tickets. We were warned not to talk about our camp experiences, or we would be brought back and never get out alive. By the time we left it was 8 P.M.; we had been "processed" all day with no food. But we got away, after an 8 km [5 mile] walk to the station.

Some prisoners managed to escape from the camps. Some escapees were caught, but others were not. The SS wanted prisoners to think that they would always be caught if they escaped. They always claimed to have caught escapees and executed them. It had to look as if no one was getting away.

A Successful Escape

On June 20, 1942, four Polish prisoners escaped from Auschwitz I. They were working in the garage of the supply depot and managed to get a hold of some SS uniforms. One dressed as an SS officer, two others as SS guards. The last one was dressed in his prison clothes and chains. In this way, they looked like SS men moving a prisoner from one camp to another. They stole a car from the garage and drove it 50 miles (80 kilometers) from the camp before abandoning it. They then sent the camp commandant a letter, jokingly apologizing for stealing the car. They were never caught.

Caught!

Hans Bonarewitz escaped from Mauthausen camp in June 1942, hiding in a wooden packing case on a truck driving out of the camp. He was caught eighteen days after he escaped. As punishment, Hans was locked in a packing case like the one he escaped in for a week, without food or water. The case was left in the square all that time, so the other prisoners could hear, and smell, his agony.

On July 30 he was taken out of the case and cleaned up. This photograph next to the packing case was taken by the SS. He was then executed in front of all of the prisoners.

Safer Inside?

Partisans fought the **Nazis** secretly, often hiding out in the forests. The Nazis knew about these groups and spent a lot of time trying to catch them. Not all of the groups would help everyone.

Roman Frister escaped from Starachowice camp one night when the camp lights were turned out during an air raid. Twenty-three prisoners made it into a nearby forest. They looked for, and found, a group of partisans to join. While Roman was washing at a stream, the partisans killed the other escapees. They were Polish partisans. The Nazis left them alone because they hated **Jews** so much that they killed any escapees. Roman went to a farm for help and was refused for fear of the partisans. So, Roman broke back into the camp and acted as if he had never tried to escape.

Going for Help

Some prisoners not only escaped, they spread the news of what was happening in the camps to the outside world. Rudolf Vrba and Alfred Wetzler, both prisoners in Auschwitz camp, escaped in April 1944. They made their way to Slovakia and told the Jewish leaders there how Jews from all over Europe were being killed in Auschwitz. Vrba had worked in the **SS** offices and had memorized the details of many of the people.

Shortly after they escaped, two more escapees from Auschwitz arrived and confirmed what Vrba and Wetzler had said. Their information was published in **Allied** newspapers and pressure was put on the Hungarian government to stop sending Hungarian Jews to Auschwitz. The **transports** stopped. The escapees saved over 170,000 Hungarian Jews.

Partisans

This photo shows some of the people who escaped to join a partisan group led by two brothers named Bielski.

A Memorable Event?

The soldiers who liberated the camps remember the horror all too clearly, but many prisoners were too sick to have clear memories of being liberated. Perec Zylberberg was part of a trainload of prisoners sent from Buchenwald to Terezín. He has only vague memories of the journey:

> *I seem to remember eating grass, leaves, bark. I lost count of the days and nights. Then I was in a building with bunks. I remember nurses and a bed to myself and a piece of bread. I was told I had* **typhus** *and was safe in a clinic. Then I remember seeing a tank outside and thinking: the Allies are here.*

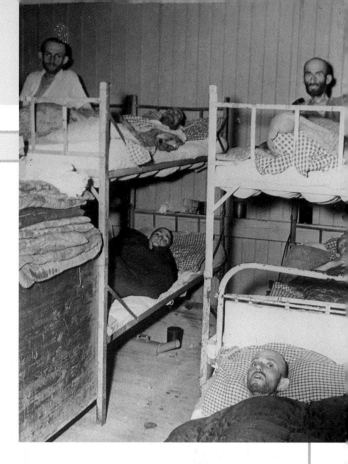

This photo shows some prisoners, after liberation, in Buchenwald infirmary. They had not been moved to Terezín by the time the SS fled.

Hidden From the SS

Israel Lau, a young prisoner in Buchenwald camp, was still alive when the SS decided to move the prisoners out ahead of the advancing U.S. soldiers. The SS marched the prisoners out on April 8, 1945. Israel's brother, Naftali, hid Israel in a pile of dead bodies, telling him to stay there until the Americans arrived, which they did on April 11. The soldiers found 21,000 people hiding with the unburied corpses, including 4,000 Jews. This shows what a huge number of dead there must have been. Naftali did not survive the march from Buchenwald.

Liberation

The last way to leave the camps was, simply, to survive long enough for Germany to lose the war. At that time the Allies, Germany's enemies, **liberated** the camps, letting the prisoners go. Most camps were liberated during April and May 1945. The Allied soldiers were stunned at what they found. They found more dead prisoners than living ones—the SS did not want to leave survivors to talk about what had been going on. Other prisoners were liberated while being marched or transported by train to new camps.

41

Roman Frister

Roman Frister was born in Bielsko-Biala, Poland, in 1928. His father was a successful lawyer. When the German army **occupied** Poland in 1939, the Fristers moved to Lvov, then to Kraków, where Roman's grandparents lived. The **Nazis** set up **ghettos** and ordered all **Jews** to move into them. Roman's grandparents, known Jews, had to go. Roman's father bought forged papers for the family and they stayed free, living in a small, damp basement room. Roman worked as a delivery boy. Later, his mother worked as a typist in a local **SS** Officers' Club.

Roman decided to get his grandparents out of the ghetto. Jews who had become Catholic were treated as Jews, but they could be buried in Catholic cemeteries, outside the ghetto. Roman got his grandparents out disguised as a priest and a nun, with Roman as the priest's assistant. Roman put his grandparents on a bus to stay with relatives in the countryside. Not long after, Roman was stopped by a patrol:

> I handed him my papers and, without being asked, also handed over my work permit. . . . There was a man lurking in a nearby doorway. The policeman holding my ID glanced at him and he nodded. "Jude" said the policeman.

Roman was forced to lead the SS to his family. His father was sent to Plaszow **concentration camp,** just outside the city. His mother tried to save the family by telling an SS officer, Wilhelm Kunde, where all their property was in return for their lives. Kunde shot her and sent Roman to Plaszow with his father.

Papers

An SS officer examines the papers of some Jews in the Kraków Ghetto.

Epidemic Diseases

Because of the poor living conditions in the ghettos, there were many outbreaks of disease. This notice, at the entrance to the Radom Ghetto in Poland, warns people coming in of the dangers of disease. Once people were moved to camps, there were no warning signs like this. The Nazis did not provide people with enough access to clean water to stay clean and disease free.

Plaszow Camp

Roman and his father were first imprisoned in Plaszow camp.

One evening during the second week in the camp, the camp commander, Amon Goeth and the chief Jewish **kapo** *came to our barracks. The* kapo *told us to hand over all our money or valuables; we had to fill Goeth's officer's cap, or else. The cap filled in half a minute. Goeth ordered the* kapo *to search a prisoner—there was money in his sock. Goeth shot him through the throat and looked around for his next victim. I was nearby, but the pistol passed me. He killed another prisoner, took his cap and left.*

Starachowice

In 1943, the Nazis decided to cut the size of Plaszow camp. Hundreds of prisoners were shot and thousands were sent to other camps. By sheer chance, Roman and his father were put on the same train, to Starachowice:

The camp was on top of a hill and other camps were scattered around nearby, their prisoners mostly a mixture of Poles and Jews. I was one of the youngest at the steelworks, making bomb casings and gun barrels. The steelwork furnaces worked around the clock and as long as they kept working we were allowed to live. My father's job was to push carts of steel mold. . . . Each cart weighed half a ton, and was always likely to come off the rails they ran on. When this happened, the guards beat the "guilty" worker until the cart was back on the rails.

Roman's father caught **typhus** and died in the hospital. Roman caught typhus, too, but survived. As the Russians closed in on Starachowice, the prisoners revolted. The camp was closed and the prisoners were sent to Auschwitz.

Auschwitz

The journey to Auschwitz was horrific:

> *A sign in our cattle car said it held twelve horses or 24 cows. Now it held 100 men. It stank and was impossible to move. The doors of the car were opened on the third day . . . we were on the "ramp" of Birkenau . . . we were lucky—we were all marched off to the showers without a **"selection."***

> *In the shower room we were ordered to undress, fold our clothes, and lay them neatly at our feet. We were inspected by a young guard with a whip. . . . The prisoner on the right saw my bleeding leg and moved away as if I was a leper. The bloody bandage wrapped around it said: the boy dies. But the officer was distracted, chose to shoot another victim. So I lived.*

A Huge Camp

These photos show Auschwitz-Birkenau from the tower on the main gate. It stretches away as far as the eye can see in all directions. It took Roman some time to understand the camp.

> *A view of the camp from the air would have showed a huge, flat, treeless stretch of land divided into rectangular strips. Each strip had about 20 barracks and a toilet block, surrounded by electrified fences. They were designed to keep the different sorts of prisoners apart, to make organized resistance harder. . . . Yet the Gypsies were kept in one section of the camp, all together, and were allowed to live as they pleased. The guards even let them go on playing their music after curfew, when the rest of us had to be in our bunks. Then, one night, I woke to silence. The Gypsies had been taken to the **gas chambers.***

Metalworking

These prisoners are in one of the metalworking workshops in Auschwitz I. This photo was taken by the SS in about 1942. It is likely that they intended it as a **propaganda** photo, to show that their prisoners were given reasonable living and working conditions.

Taking a Chance

Sometimes the **SS** came to the camp to look for replacement workers. Roman volunteered to work as a lathe operator— a job he knew nothing about. He was taken off to a steel plant in Auschwitz III:

Now I would live while they had a use for me. But what would happen when I had to work my first lathe? In the morning we were kicked awake and kicked into line. We walked to the factory. At 6 A.M. I was faced with my first lathe. It bared its teeth at me, as if it was about to tear me apart. The foreman brought me a blueprint in German. I didn't understand the words or the diagrams. I looked around. The work force was huge. Dozens of machines stood in ruler-straight lines, each with an operator, each working. The foreman stepped up behind me, "Having trouble with the blueprint?"

Roman: *No sir.*

Foreman: *Your daily quota is 84 parts; anything over that you'll get extra rations, any less a whipping.*

He moved on.

I took a metal rod and put it in the machine. I pressed a black button. Nothing happened. I pressed a red one. Nothing happened. The prisoner on my left said in Polish: "Hey yid, your God sure isn't going to work that lathe for you."

Roman: *I suppose not.*

Polish prisoner: *You're not the first or the last to try this. Tomorrow they'll make soap out of you. You know that's what they do to dead **Jews,** don't you?*

Roman: *At least I'll leave the world a cleaner place.*

He liked the answer. Then he lent over, studied the blueprint, and showed me what to do. He set it up for me saying: "Everything here is automatic and very simple. Watch me closely." He taught me what to do. So I became a live lathe operator. His name was Kurt Kolonko and he saved my life.

Giving Out Clothing

Here, clothing is being given out at Mauthausen. The prisoners had to undress and re-dress in the yard. Even if they arrived in Mauthausen from another camp, prisoners had to go through the whole arrivals process, including being issued a different uniform.

Arrival at Mauthausen

In January 1945, the steel plant was shut down and evacuated. Roman was one of the prisoners taken to Mauthausen:

"Let's go! Let's go!" yelled the **Nazis.** *"Clothes off and against the wall, let's go!" I was out of my clothes in less than twenty seconds. The slowest had no space at the wall, and were beaten. . . . "Prepare for a shower!" We had come from Auschwitz, where the showers meant the* **gas chambers.** *Were the Nazis going to kill us? Not yet. Ice-cold water was sprayed from fire hoses aimed at our naked bodies. The powerful jet pounded my body, threw me against the wall. Blood ran down my face and froze there. The water had already turned to ice on my body. By the time they had finished there were dozens of corpses in the yard.*

We were herded through a gate into a second square. Here we were registered. . . . My bare feet were frozen to the ground. At last I was given a tin bracelet with my new number on it. "Guard it like gold," said the **kapo.** *"You're a dead man without it." He gave me a kick in the direction of the showers. No, these were not gas chambers, either. Real water came out of them. I didn't notice it was boiling hot. That night, my body was covered in blisters. . . . Out of the shower I was thrown a shirt too small to button and trousers that were far too big. Jackets, we were told, were only for prisoners who had been here awhile.*

Working

Roman nearly gave up in Mauthausen. No one was working in their part of the camp, and those who did not work were more likely to be killed. Then he was taken to a sub-camp near Vienna, Austria, that made tank engines:

> There were 1,500 of us at morning **roll call.** The kapos and **SS** guards treated us less harshly because they were told we had economic value. The food was still bad, but we each had our own bunk with a straw mattress and a blanket. . . . It was easy to get used to these conditions.

Death March

Then, one day there was a change:

> One roll call, instead of being sent to work, we were given a loaf of sticky black bread, a packet of red beet jam, and a blanket. The camp **commandant** made a speech: "Prisoners! The **Third Reich** does not desert those who serve it, willingly or unwillingly. The Bolshevik hordes are nearing Vienna. We will march on foot to a safer destination, where you will work again." We marched in perfect formation through Vienna. . . . As we went, the column fell apart. Prisoners fell behind, were left there. The SS didn't care anymore. After nine days hundreds of prisoners were missing and corpses lined the road. We arrived with 322 prisoners out of 1,020.

Roman ended up in a hospital ward again at Mauthausen and was there when the camp was **liberated.** He became a journalist and emigrated to Israel in 1957. Roman became a reporter for the Israeli newspaper *Ha'aretz.* He published his autobiography, *Self Portrait with a Scar,* in 1993. It was translated into English as *The Cap: The Price of a Life,* in 1999.

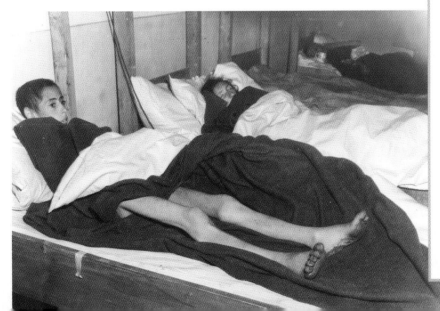

Surviving

These prisoners, who were photographed in Buchenwald camp after liberation, survived death marches and train evacuations. However, many prisoners were near death from starvation, brutality, and disease when they were liberated. Soldiers and aid workers who arrived at liberation had to watch hundreds of prisoners die because they were too far gone to be saved.

Camps

This is a list of the main camps of several kinds in **Greater Germany** and Poland. Most of these camps are mentioned in the text or appear on the map on page 5. The list does not include all of the sub-camps, prisoner-of-war camps, or holding camps. Nor does it include camps in the rest of **occupied** Europe.

Death camps
Belzec
Chelmno
Sobibor
Treblinka

Combined camps
Auschwitz-Birkenau
Majdanek

Concentration camps
Bergen-Belsen
Buchenwald
Dachau
Flossenbürg
Gross Rosen
Gunskirchen
Gusen
Lublin
Mauthausen
Natzweiler
Neuengamme
Ohrdruf
Sachsenhausen
   [Oranienburg]
Plaszow
Ravensbrück
Stutthof
Terezín [Theresienstadt]

Labor camps in Poland
Blizyn
Bochnia
Budzyn
Deblin
Gliwice
Izbica
Katowice
Koluszki
Mielec
Monowitz
Otoczno
Piotrkow
Poniatowa
Pustkow
Rzeszow
Skarzysko-Kamienna
Sosnowiec
Starachowice
Szebnie
Trawniki
Zawiercie

Labor camps in Germany
Bautzen
Braunschweig
Dora
Dresden
Flössberg
Hannover
Hessenthal
Krawinkel
Lieberose
Ludwigslust
Nordhausen
Rehmsdorf
Schlieben
Sonneberg
Spaichingen
Treglitz
Wiehagen

Timeline

1933

January 30	Adolf Hitler comes to power in Germany as Chancellor.
February 27	A fire breaks out at the *Reichstag*, the German Parliament. The **Nazis** blame the **Communists** and produce a Dutch communist who confesses.
February 28	German President Hindenburg's decree, "For the Protection of the People and the State," allows for the creation of **concentration camps.** The Nazis persuade Hindenburg to pass the decree to fight what they called the "Communist threat."
March 17	The **SS** (short for *Schutzstaffel*, "security staff") is set up as Hitler's bodyguard.
March 21	Dachau, the first Nazi concentration camp, is set up. Concentration camps and **labor camps** are set up steadily after this.
April 26	The **Gestapo**—Nazi secret police— is set up.
May 2	Trade unions are banned in Germany.
July 14	**Political** parties other than the Nazi Party are banned in Germany.

1934

April 20	Heinrich Himmler is placed in charge of the Gestapo.
July 20	The SS is no longer under the control of the German army.
August 2	Hitler makes himself *Führer*, sole leader of Germany.

1935

September 15	The Nuremberg Laws are passed against German **Jews.**

1936

March 29	The SS grows to 3,500 men.
June 17	Himmler is placed in charge of all police departments.

1937

July 16	Buchenwald concentration camp is set up.

1938

March 13	Germany takes over Austria.
June 25	Jewish doctors can no longer treat non-Jewish patients.
August 8	Mauthausen concentration camp is set up.
October 28	The first Jews are deported from Poland by the Polish government.
November 9	*Kristallnacht* takes place. Nazi-led violence against Jews includes burning synagogues and looting Jewish stores and homes.

1939

August 28	Rationing is introduced. It covers food and essential items like clothes and gasoline.
September 1	Germany invades Poland and takes immediate action against Polish Jews.
September 3	Britain and France declare war on Germany.
September 17	The Soviet Union invades Poland from the east.
September 28	Germany and the Soviet Union split Poland between them.
November 30	The Soviet Union invades Finland.

1940

February 12	The first **Jews** are deported from their homes in Germany and taken to **ghettos** in Poland.
April 9	Germany invades Denmark and Norway.
April 27	Himmler builds a camp at Auschwitz.
April 30	A large ghetto is set up in the Polish city of Lodz. All Jews from the city and the surrounding area are sent there. More ghettos are planned in other Polish cities for Polish Jews, and then for Jews from other lands controlled by Germany.
May 10	Germany invades Belgium, France, Luxembourg, and Holland.
November 15	The Warsaw Ghetto is set up in Poland.

1941

April 6	Germany invades Yugoslavia and Greece.
June 22	Germany invades the Soviet Union and begins killing Jews in large numbers as the German army moves through the Soviet Union.
September 1	All German Jews over the age of six have to wear a yellow Star of David with "*Jude*" written in black on it.
From September	Mass gassings at Auschwitz begin with Soviet prisoners-of-war and continue. They focus on Jews and become more regular from January 1942.
October 10	The Terezín Ghetto is set up in Czechoslovakia.
October 16	Mass deportation of Jews to Poland begins.
October 28	10,000 Jews are **selected** and killed at Kovno Ghetto in Lithuania.
December 7	Japan bombs Pearl Harbor.
December 8	The first group of Jews are gassed at Chelmno **death camp** in Poland.
December 11	Germany declares war on the United States.

1942

January 20	The Wannsee Conference is called to discuss the "Final Solution" to the "Jewish Problem."
January 21	The United Partisan Organization, a Jewish resistance group, is set up in the Vilna Ghetto in Lithuania.
March 1	The first deportation of Jews to Sobibor death camp in Poland takes place.
March 17	The first deportation of Jews to Belzec death camp in Poland takes place.
March 26	The first deportations to Auschwitz-Birkenau and to the Majdanek death camps take place.
March 27	The first deportation of French Jews to Auschwitz takes place.
March 30–May 1	**Allies** bomb Cologne, Germany.
July 15	The first group of Dutch Jews are deported to Auschwitz.
July 22	Daily deportations to Treblinka camp in Poland from the Warsaw Ghetto begin.
October 4	Himmler orders that all Jews in **concentration camps** are to be sent to Auschwitz-Birkenau to be killed.

1943

January 18	There are four days of unrest in the Warsaw Ghetto because of deportations.
March 17	Bulgaria refuses to deport Bulgarian Jews.
April 17	Hungary refuses to deport Hungarian Jews.
April 19	The Warsaw Ghetto revolt begins. The **SS** moves back into the city.
June 11	Himmler orders all remaining ghettos to be emptied and their inhabitants killed.

1944

March 23	The deportation of Greek Jews begins.
April 7	Two Jews escape from Auschwitz and reach Brostalvia in Slovakia. News of the camp can no longer be ignored in the west.
May 15	Mass deportation and gassing of Hungarian Jews begins.
From June	Death marches from camps in Poland begins.
June 6	Allied troops land in Normandy, France.
August 4	Anne Frank and her family are arrested in Amsterdam. Anne's diaries of her experiences in hiding before this arrest became famous after the war.

1945

January 17	The final death march from Auschwitz-Birkenau takes place.
January 27	Soviet troops reach Auschwitz.
April 11	U.S. troops reach Buchenwald camp.
April 15	British troops reach Belsen camp.
April 29	U.S. troops reach Dachau camp. Russian troops reach Berlin camp.
April 30	Hitler commits suicide in Berlin.
May 5	U.S. troops reach Mauthausen camp.
May 7	Germany surrenders to the Allies.
November 20	The Nuremberg trials of Nazi war criminals begin. The first war criminals are executed in October 1946.

Glossary

Ally country that fought against Nazi Germany in World War II

Aryan word used by the Nazis to mean people with northern European ancestors, without any ancestors from what they called "inferior" races, such as Poles, Slavs, or Jews. Aryans were usually blonde, blue-eyed, and sturdy.

asocial Nazi term for people who did not support the Nazi state. Asocials could be drunks, people who would not work, homosexuals, or members of a religious group whose beliefs might make them oppose the Nazis.

blockälteste female prisoner put in charge of a barracks; men were called *blockältesters*

commandant person in charge of a camp

Communist person who believes that a country should be governed by the people of that country for the good of everyone in it. They believe private property is wrong, including owning a home or a business. The state should own everything and run everything, giving the people the things they need.

concentration camp prison camp set up by the Nazis under a special law that meant that the prisoners were never tried and were never given a release date. The Nazis could put anyone in these camps, for any reason or none, for as long as they wanted.

crematorium place with special ovens for burning bodies

death camp camp set up by the Nazis to murder as many people, most of them Jewish, as quickly and cheaply as possible. Most of the victims were gassed.

Einsatzgruppen special units of the German army set up by the Nazis. These units went into eastern Europe at the same time as the army. Their job was supposedly to round up and kill civilians who were a danger to the Reich. In fact, they were told to kill Jews.

gas chamber large room, often disguised as showers, that the Nazis filled with people. When the room was full the Nazis pumped gas into it, to kill the people inside.

Gestapo secret police set up by the Nazis in 1933

ghetto area of a town or city, walled or fenced off from the rest of the city, where Jewish people were forced to live

Greater Germany term used to mean the combined lands of Germany, Austria, Czechoslovakia, and parts of Poland from 1939 to 1945. However, the Nazis also used it to mean all of the lands they controlled in Europe.

Holocaust huge destruction or sacrifice. When it appears with a capital "H," it refers to the deliberate attempt by the Nazi government in Germany to destroy all of the Jewish people in their power.

Jehovah's Witnesses religious group that was especially persecuted by the Nazis because members refused to swear an oath of loyalty to Hitler

Jew (Jewish) someone who follows the Jewish faith. The Nazis also called people Jews if they had Jewish ancestors, even if they had changed their faith.

Judenfrei "Jew Free;" a place with no Jewish people living there

kapo prisoner who is put in charge of other prisoners when they are working

labor camp camp set up by the Nazis that was a prison that used the prisoners as cheap labor

liberated used in this book to mean a place, especially a concentration camp, being freed from the control of the SS. Camps were liberated by Allied soldiers.

menorah seven- or nine-branched candlestick used in the Jewish religious festival Hanukkah

Nazi member of the Nazi Party. Nazi is short for *Nationalsozialistische Deutsche Arbeiterpartei*, the National Socialist German Workers' Party.

occupied used in this book to mean a country that has been captured by Germany and is ruled by Nazis supported by the German army

partisan someone who fights an army that has invaded and taken over their country

political having to do with ideas and actions of government; person arrested for opposing Nazi ideas or actions

prisoner functionary prisoner, usually a German criminal, put in charge of other prisoners as a *kapo* or *blockältester*

propaganda information and ideas that are worded and presented so that people will accept and believe them, even if they are not true

quarantine to keep people who might be carrying a disease away from other people so they will not spread that disease. Used by the Nazis to refer to the first few days or weeks people spent in a new camp. The Nazis said the quarantine was medical, but it was really to terrorize the prisoners into obedience.

race group of people with the same ancestors

Red Cross organization set up to give medical aid and other help in wartime or other times of crisis

resettlement taking people away from one place and making them settle somewhere else. Jewish people who were moved to the ghettos and then to the camps by the Nazis were promised they would be "resettled" in the east.

roll call count of all prisoners in a camp, usually in the morning and evening

sanitation providing clean water and removing waste and sewage to prevent disease

SS (short for *Schutzstaffel*) security staff. The SS began as Hitler's personal bodyguard. Later, they ran concentration camps and death camps. Everyone in the SS swore loyalty to Hitler, rather than Germany.

selection used in this book to refer to the SS process in the camps of choosing which people to kill

TB tuberculosis; an infectious disease, mostly of the lungs, that can be fatal

Third Reich "the third empire." The Nazis saw their rule as the third German empire, with Hitler as the emperor, or *Führer*.

transport used in this book to refer to a trainload of people being sent to the camps

typhus disease caused by dirty conditions and spread by polluted water, usually polluted with sewage. Typhus causes high temperatures, rashes, vomiting, and diarrhea. It can be fatal.

undesirable word used by the Nazis to describe any person that they did not approve of

Winter Aid charity run by the Nazis to raise money to help the poor of Germany

Further Reading

Frank, Anne. *Diary of a Young Girl.* Columbus, Ohio: Prentice Hall, 1993.

Shuter, Jane. *Auschwitz.* Chicago: Heinemann Library, 1999.

Tames, Richard. *Anne Frank.* Chicago: Heinemann Library, 1998.

Tames, Richard. *Adolf Hitler.* Chicago: Heinemann Library, 1998.

Whittock, Martyn. *Hitler & National Socialism.* Chicago: Heinemann Library, 1996.

Wiesel, Elie. *Night.* New York: Bantam Books, 1982.

Willoughby, Susan. *The Holocaust.* Chicago: Heinemann Library, 2000.

Sources

The author and publisher gratefully acknowledge the publications from which written sources in this book are drawn. In some cases, the wording or sentence structure has been simplified to make the material appropriate for a school readership.

Adelsberger, Lucie. *Auschwitz: A Doctor's Story.* Boston: Northeastern University Press, 1995. (p. 17)

Beon, Yves. *Planet Dora: A Memoir of the Holocaust and the Birth of the Space Age.* Boulder, Colo.: Westview Press, 1998. (pp. 22, 33)

DeSilva, Cara (editor). *In Memory's Kitchen: A Legacy From the Women of Terezín.* Northvale, N.J.: Jason Aronson, 1996. (p. 23)

Dwork, Deborah and Robert Jan van Pelt. *Auschwitz: 1270 to Present.* Scranton, Penn.: W. W. Norton & Company, 1996. (p. 30)

Engelmann, Bernt. *In Hitler's Germany.* Westminster, Md.: Schocken Books, Incorporated, 1988. (pp. 12, 38)

Fénelon, Fania. *Playing For Time.* Syracuse, N.Y.: Syracuse University Press, 1997. (pp. 16, 36)

Frister, Roman. *The Cap: The Price of a Life.* Cambridge, UK: Grove Books, Limited, 1999. (pp. 40, 42–47)

Gilbert, Martin. *The Boys: The Story of 732 Young Concentration Camp Survivors.* New York: Henry Holt & Company, 1997. (p. 41)

Gryn, Hugo. *Chasing Shadows.* East Rutherford, N.J.: Viking Penguin, 2000. (pp. 14, 19, 30)

Klee, Ernst, Willi Dressen, and Volker Riess. *The Good Old Days: The Holocaust as Seen by its Perpetrators and Bystanders.* Old Saybrook, Conn.: William S. Konecky Associated, Inc., 1997. (pp. 13, 35)

Klein, Gerda Weissmann. *All But My Life.* New York: Hill & Wang, 1995. (pp. 15, 23)

Noakes, J. and G. Pridham. *Nazism, 1919–1945.* Exeter, UK: University of Exeter Press, 1991. (p. 38)

Novac, Ana. *The Beautiful Days of My Youth: My Six Months in Auschwitz and Plaszow.* New York: Henry Holt & Company, 1992. (pp. 7, 8, 15, 16, 20, 23, 26, 27)

Sobolewicz, Tadeusz. *But I Survived.* Oswiecim, Poland: Auschwitz State Museum, 1998. (pp. 11, 21, 29)

Places of Interest and Websites

C.A.N.D.L.E.S. Holocaust Museum (Children of Auschwitz Nazi Deadly Labs Experiments)
1532 South Third Street
Terre Haute, IN 47802
Visitor information: (812) 234-7881
Website: *http://www.candles-museum.org*

El Paso Holocaust Museum and Study Center
401 Wallenberg Drive
El Paso, TX 79912
Visitor information: (915) 833-5656
Website: *http://www.huntel.com/~ht2/holocaust.html*

Florida Holocaust Museum
55 Fifth Street South
St. Petersburg, FL 33701
Visitor information: (727) 820-0100
Website: *http://www.flholocaustmuseum.org*

Museum of Jewish Heritage: A Living Memorial to the Holocaust
18 First Place
Battery Park City
New York, NY 10004
Visitor information: (212) 509-6130
Website: *http://www.mjhnyc.org*

United States Holocaust Memorial Museum
100 Raoul Wallenberg Place, SW
Washington, D.C. 20024
Visitor information: (202) 488-0400
Website: *http://www.ushmm.org*

Website warning

1. Almost all Holocaust websites have been designed for adult users. They can contain horrifying and upsetting information and pictures.
2. Some people wish to minimize the Holocaust, or even deny that it happened at all. Some of their websites pretend to be delivering unbiased facts and information. To be sure you are getting accurate information, it is always best to use an officially recognized site such as the ones listed on this page.
3. If you plan to visit a Holocaust website, ask an adult to view the site with you.

Disclaimer
All the Internet addresses (URLs) given in this book were valid at the time of going to press. However, due to the dynamic nature of the Internet, some addresses may have changed, or sites may have ceased to exist since publication. While the author and publisher regret any inconvenience this may cause readers, no responsibility for any such changes can be accepted by either the author or the publisher.

Index